STATHEAD SPORTS

STATHEAD
HOCKEY
How Data Changed the Sport

by Hans Hetrick

COMPASS POINT BOOKS
a capstone imprint

Stathead Sports is published
by Compass Point Books, a Capstone imprint
1710 Roe Crest Drive, North Mankato, Minnesota 56003
www.mycapstone.com

Library of Congress Cataloging-in-Publication Data is available on the Library
of Congress website.
ISBN 978-1-5435-1446-9 (library binding)
ISBN 978-1-5435-1450-6 (paperback)
ISBN 978-1-5435-1454-4 (eBook PDF)

Editorial Credits
Nick Healy, editor; Terri Poburka, designer; Eric Gohl, media researcher;
Laura Manthe, production specialist

Photo Credits
Alamy: H.S. Photos, 18; Dreamstime: Jerry Coli, 33; Getty Images: Bruce Bennett,
25, 36, Doug Griffin, 19, Melchior DiGiacomo, 16; Newscom: Cal Sport Media/
Andy Blenkush, 28, Cal Sport Media/Chris Szagola, cover, Cal Sport Media/
Mike Wulf, 10–11, 26, Icon SMI/Jeanine Leech, 38, Icon Sports Photos, 12, Icon
Sportswire/Robin Alam, 15, Reuters/Joe Traver, 31, USA Today Sports/Perry
Nelson, 9, ZUMA Press/Darryl Dyck, 42, ZUMA Press/Dean Beattie, 4, ZUMA
Press/Rene Johnston, 23; Shutterstock: Inked Pixels, back cover

Design Elements: Shutterstock

Printed in the United States of America.
PA017

TABLE OF CONTENTS

AN ARGUMENT FOR ADVANCED STATS

▶ Mikhail Grabovski was hardly a superstar for the Maple Leafs, but by some measures, he was too effective to let go.

Are hockey statistics something to shout about? You would surely think so if you had been listening to Steve Simmons during a radio interview with Tyler Dellow several years ago. Simmons, a sportswriter and radio commentator in Toronto, objected to Dellow's claims about a former Toronto Maple Leafs player named Mikhail Grabovski. And Simmons objected loudly.

Simmons blew his top when Dellow, a blogger and believer in advanced statistics, suggested that the Maple Leafs should not have let go of Grabovski. The two were discussing the team's need for a third-line center at the time. Grabovski had once handled those duties for the Leafs, who were coming off an unsuccessful season.

Dellow said, "The Leafs created this problem a little bit because they got rid of Grabovski."

Simmons spoke up and half-shouted, "Oh-oh-oh, I have to interrupt here. Grabovski is a bad player. He's a third-line center who plays lone-wolf hockey. You can throw your stats out the window on this guy. Every team that's ever had him was frustrated by him."

But Dellow wasn't about to throw stats out the window. He was among the believers in new ways of analyzing players and teams. He replied to Simmons with this question: "Why were they frustrated by him?"

"Because he doesn't produce!" Simmons barked, his voice still raised.

"His teams produce when he's on the ice. What do you mean he doesn't produce?" Dellow said. "When Grabovski's on the ice, his teams put up goals. Isn't that kind of the objective of hockey? To score more goals than the other team?"

Simmons did not challenge that particular point. He did not offer evidence that Dellow was wrong. Simmons said loudly, "Talk to the people on the hockey team! Throw your stats out the window for a minute! Talk to the people who run the hockey team."

With Grabovski, the Leafs had made the National Hockey League (NHL) playoffs after the 2012–13 season. But the Leafs hadn't kept Grabovski around. He signed with the Washington Capitals for the next season. Without him in 2013–14, the Leafs missed the playoffs.

Dellow raised this issue and used a simple stat to back his point. He said, "And how did the Leafs do in the playoffs this year? They let Grabovski go and didn't make it. Look at his numbers: When Grabovski was on the ice this year, Washington got 57.5 percent of the goals. You tell me, would the Leafs have benefitted from having a player that helps them get 57.5 percent of the goals when he's on the ice? I think they would have."

Still sounding angry, Simmons said, "You're telling me in today's NHL that Mikhail Grabovski makes a difference?"

"Yeah," Dellow replied.

Simmons pressed on, saying, "You're telling me every general manager in the league is wrong and you're right?"

Dellow went back to the numbers. He said, "There's a lot of general managers in hockey that could have used 800 minutes of hockey in which their team scored 57.5 percent of the goals."

Surely this argument was great fun for radio listeners.

But the flare-up between Simmons and Dellow was just one battle in a long war between the old school and the new school. The new school, including Tyler Dellow, was revolutionizing the way people look at hockey. They were using advanced stats, or hockey analytics, to produce completely fresh insights into the game.

Folks like Steve Simmons believed in old school, traditional hockey. They laughed off the new advanced stats community. The old school dismissed advanced stats every chance they could. They labeled them "fancy stats" and hurled a "just watch the game, nerds" at anyone who dared bring up a new statistic.

The old school saw no place for the new school in pro hockey. They held advanced stats on the fringes of the hockey world for a long time. But it was only a matter of time before the hockey world embraced the possibilities of advanced stats. Soon the NHL started putting experts in advanced stats to work. Statistics, it seemed, were changing the game—and that change continues today.

Perhaps the oldest and simplest way to judge a pro hockey player is total points. A player gets a point when he scores a goal or gets an assist. Assists are awarded to the last two offensive players to handle the puck before it gets to the scorer, as long as the other team doesn't control the puck between passes.

During the 2016–17 season, second-year pro Connor McDavid reached 100 points. The Edmonton Oilers' center scored 30 goals and dished out 70 assists. He was only 19 years old when that season began, and fans of the Oilers had high hopes for his future. The next season McDavid netted 41 goals and finished with 108 points. He showed that he belonged among the NHL's superstars.

McDavid's success also reminded fans of an earlier star who wore an Oilers sweater. In the 1980s, Wayne Gretzky became known simply as The Great One. He collected 212 points in 1981–82, making him the first player to ever top 200. He scored an astonishing 92 goals that season. Hockey fans had never seen anything like him.

That was the first of four seasons in which the superstar finished with more than 200 points. In 1985–86, he thrilled Edmonton fans by scoring 53 goals and dishing out 163 assists. That gave him 215 points. It's a single-season record that seems unlikely to be broken.

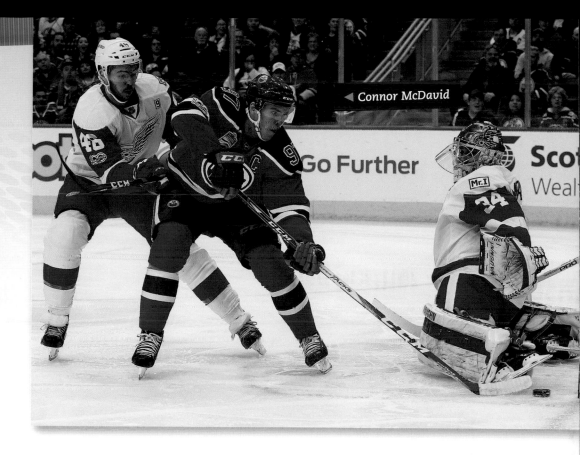

◄ Connor McDavid

Gretzky holds the NHL's career scoring record with 2,857 points. His total includes 894 goals and 1,963 assists, which are both records.

Most Goals in a Season

RANK	PLAYER	TEAM	GOALS	SEASON
1	Wayne Gretzky	Oilers	92	1981–82
2	Wayne Gretzky	Oilers	87	1983–84
3	Brett Hull	Blues	86	1990–91
4	Mario Lemieux	Penguins	85	1988–89
5	Temmu Selanne	Jets	76	1992–93

CHAPTER 1

OLD VERSUS NEW

The advanced stats revolution was led by a group of fans in love with hockey and fascinated by statistics. About a decade ago, advanced stats blogs, like the one Tyler Dellow created, began turning up all over the Internet. These bloggers were not hockey insiders. They were accountants, lawyers, engineers, and software programmers. And they were huge fans of hockey.

People like Dellow and other serious followers of the game laid the foundation for today's thriving hockey analytics community. At the beginning, just a few "statheads" kept busy by breaking down hockey statistics. These trailblazers inspired other math-loving fans. Before long, a small army of hockey number-crunchers was finding new insights about their favorite sport.

The Old School Backlash

It might come as no surprise that the advanced stats revolution was met with resistance. A lot of advanced stats theories threatened long-held hockey beliefs and traditions. Traditions die hard, and the NHL honors its traditions more than most sports. After all, the league has been passing around Lord Stanley's Cup since 1893.

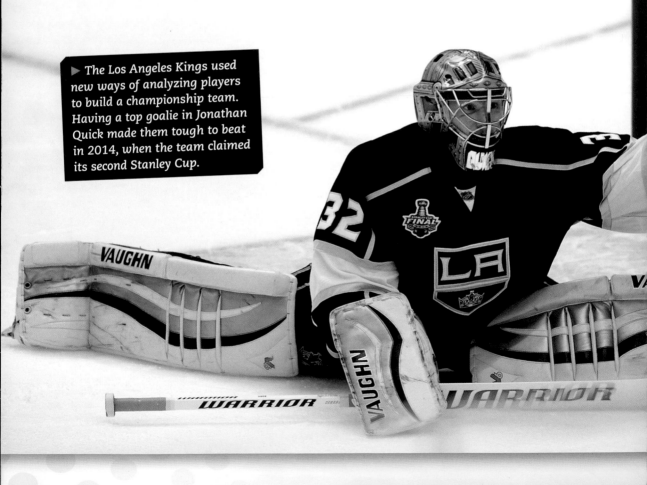

▶ The Los Angeles Kings used new ways of analyzing players to build a championship team. Having a top goalie in Jonathan Quick made them tough to beat in 2014, when the team claimed its second Stanley Cup.

Most NHL general managers, coaches, and sportswriters rejected advanced stats instantly. These insiders didn't think they were doing anything wrong. They were the experts after all. The insiders had some questions: What did some accountant in Halifax, Nova Scotia, know about which defenseman is getting paid too much? Why would an NHL coach listen to a lawyer from Buffalo about the best power-play line?

The advanced stats bloggers were true outsiders. When they first started knocking on the door, nobody answered. They would have to earn their way into mainstream hockey.

The New School Persists

The advanced stats gang didn't seem to mind the cold shoulder. They loved their work. They dug in and stayed true to their mission. As the winters passed, the advanced stats analysts continued to develop and refine their ideas. Their theories became more practical, and their predictions very often turned out to be correct.

Despite resistance from hockey's power-brokers, some hockey insiders started taking an interest in hockey analytics. After all, forward-thinking general managers and coaches are always searching for an edge over opponents. Advanced stats had the potential to give them that edge. General managers could use advanced statistics to draft or sign better or overlooked players. Coaches could use advanced statistics to find favorable on-ice matchups and strategies.

A few NHL teams, including the Chicago Blackhawks and the Los Angeles Kings, put advanced stats to use before the rest of the league. Team officials didn't talk much about it. If the other teams didn't want to use advanced stats, all the better for the Blackhawks and the Kings. The Blackhawks won the Stanley Cup in 2010, 2013, and 2015. The Kings took the trophy in 2012 and 2014.

In the offseason before the 2014–15 season, advanced stats suddenly gained traction. Experts in new stats became an essential part of the NHL. Among some hockey followers, that time period became known as the "Summer of Analytics." The advanced stats revolution went mainstream. Several teams hired experts in new stats to help in their front offices. With input from these new experts, teams began to reshape their rosters.

▲ Toews hoisted the Cup after his Blackhawks topped the Tampa Bay Lightning in 2015.

Since then, advanced stats have proven their worth in the NHL. They became a hot topic in the sports media. And advanced stats have provided new ways for fans to boast or complain about their favorite teams.

CHAPTER 2

IF YOU CAN'T BEAT 'EM, HIRE 'EM

▲ The Soviet Union's Aleksandr Maltsev (left) and Canada's Red Berenson raced to the puck during the 1972 Summit Series, a landmark in hockey's evolution.

Hockey's advanced stats revolution started long before the Summer of Analytics. Work with statistics goes all the way back to the 1940s. Dick Irvin Sr., Hall of Fame Montreal Canadiens coach, hired Allan Roth to keep statistics. Roth, like today's advanced stats crew, was a complete outsider. He sold men's ties during the day.

Together, Irvin and Roth came up with a statistic called plus-minus. The stat is the number of goals scored for a team minus the number of goals against a team while any certain player is on the ice. The Canadiens kept the stat secret for more than 20 years. Finally, the NHL officially added plus-minus to the stat sheet for the 1967–68 season.

After a couple years with the Canadiens, Roth was hired by Branch Rickey, the man who signed Jackie Robinson, to work for the Brooklyn Dodgers. Allan Roth was the first full-time statistician in pro sports.

The most famous statistician in all of sports, Bill James, is a baseball expert, but he played a big role in starting modern hockey's advanced stats revolution. Many early advanced stats analysts credit James' work as their main role model. "James was my inspiration," wrote Rob Vollman, author of *Hockey Abstract*.

"Extremely well-worn copies of *Baseball Abstract* were among the only books I ever pulled off the shelf in my youth. Like James, I naturally viewed the game (and the world) through a statistical lens, and I loved

breaking down and organizing every element of that sport in an objective fashion."

In 1972 a group of Canadian NHL All-Stars squared off against the national team of the Soviet Union (USSR). They called the matchup the Summit Series. The Canadians were expected to dominate the Big Red Machine, as the Soviets (Russians) were known. To Canada's surprise, the USSR crushed Canada 7-3 in the first game. Canada came back to win four and tie one of the eight games in a hotly contested series.

The Summit Series sparked a huge interest in Russian hockey and their coach Anatoly Tarasov, known as the father of Russian hockey. Everyone wanted to know

Russia's hockey secrets. Tarasov's book, *Road to Olympus*, became a popular read. In the book, Tarasov introduced the idea of zone entries and zone exits, a concept picked up later by modern advanced stats analysts. He also pioneered a unique, fluid style of play and many training techniques.

Interestingly, Tarasov took many concepts from a book called *The Hockey Handbook*, written by a Canadian named Lloyd Percival. Tarasov used *The Hockey Handbook* to help build the USSR's Big Red Machine, but Percival's ideas had been ignored in North America for decades. Way back in 1951, Percival was using an early form of the Corsi stat, which records puck possession, and he

▲ Soviet coach Anatoly Tarasov led the USSR to three gold medals in Olympic hockey but lost to the U.S.A. in 1980.

was tracking pass locations and their connection to scoring chances.

Before the 1997–98 season, the NHL introduced real-time scoring statistics (RTSS). RTSS gave the early advanced stats bloggers the information they needed to start their revolution. RTSS provided them with player points per minute and player ice-time in even-strength play, on penalty kills, and on power plays.

The Online Rush

Advanced stats started to appear on the Internet around 2000. The stat revolution really took off around the time of the 2004–05 NHL lockout, when a whole season was canceled while owners and players battled over a new contract. In 2004 Iain Fyffe founded the Hockey Analysis Group (HAG). HAG was an online discussion group that included groundbreaking analysts like Rob Vollman and Gabriel Desjardins. Around 2007 Desjardins built one of the first online databases with non-traditional statistics.

Not long after HAG came together, a group of Edmonton Oilers fans started *Oilogosphere*. The website was the birthplace of shot-based statistics, including Corsi and Fenwick, which both track a team's shots and their opponents' shots. Through the *Oilogosphere* blogs, analysts like Tyler Dellow and Timothy Barnes figured out how to use shot-based statistics to grade teams and players.

By 2009 the Internet was teeming with so many advanced stats blogs it was impossible to keep track of them. The army of number-crunchers was pushing hockey advanced stats forward at an incredible pace. By the time the Summer of Analytics arrived, there were plenty of great analysts available for NHL teams to hire.

Hockey Gets Advanced

During the Summer of Analytics in 2014, NHL teams started snatching up advanced stats bloggers to work in their front offices. The NHL realized that without the mind of a great advanced stats analyst they wouldn't be able to compete.

Every year the NHL sees hiring and firings among coaches and general managers, and often the names of those hired and fired are familiar. Coach A gets fired by one team but hired by another. In that way, coaches and front-office staff often seem to be recycled.

But the offseason before the 2014–15 season proved to be an unusual one in the NHL. People who had made their names online or in print began getting offers from pro teams. NHL teams wanted to tap into news ways of seeing the game.

Within a few months, several teams brought bloggers and other statheads into their front offices. Those teams included the Carolina Hurricanes, Edmonton Oilers, Florida Panthers, Toronto Maple Leafs, and Washington Capitals.

Tyler Dellow, of the *MC79hockey* blog and a popular presence on Twitter, had once seemed like a serious outsider, like when he was being shouted at during that memorable radio interview. He was a fan of the Oilers, but he also criticized the team often online. Still, the team hired him to help with analyzing players.

The Florida Panthers hired Brian Macdonald, a researcher and blogger. The Carolina Hurricanes hired Eric Tulsky of the *Outnumbered* blog, while the Washington Capitals snapped up Timothy Barnes of a site called *Irreverent Oilers Fan*. The Maple Leafs brought in two new-school stat experts—Darryl Metcalf of *Extraskater.com* and Rob Pettapiece of *Buzzing the Net*.

The people teams hired that summer were true outsiders. Macdonald was at West Point Military Academy teaching for the Mathematical Sciences Department. Tulsky was working as a chemist. Barnes was a financial analyst living in Chicago.

Suddenly, these guys had their dream jobs. After years analyzing statistics for free, they were getting paid by NHL teams to help them win the Stanley Cup. The new school had finally graduated.

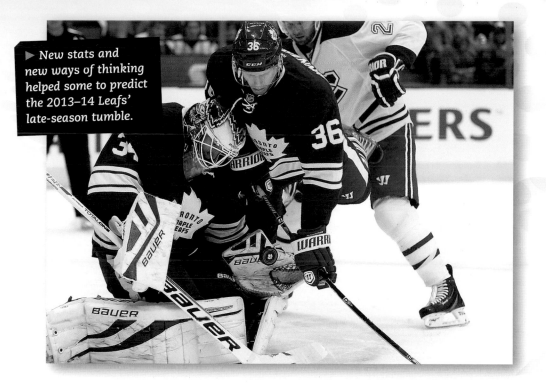

▶ New stats and new ways of thinking helped some to predict the 2013–14 Leafs' late-season tumble.

Collapse of the Maple Leafs

Toronto may not be the capital of Canada, but it is the capital of hockey. It is the home of the Hockey Hall of Fame. It is also the home of one of the NHL's most popular teams, the Maple Leafs. Also, Toronto is home to an almost round-the-clock hockey media machine. Nothing fanned the flames of the feud between insiders and statheads more than the fate of the 2013–14 Leafs.

The Maple Leafs jumped out to an unexpected hot start, and they became the big story of the season. The advanced stats bunch wasn't afraid to ruin Toronto's party. They predicted a terrible fall for Toronto's team, and hockey's capital city didn't like it one bit. The fans didn't like the thought that their team was going to crash and burn. And the Toronto sports media put advanced stats on trial. Old school versus new school debates dominated the talk shows and the sports blogs.

The Maple Leafs organization acted in direct opposition to all established advanced stats wisdom. They seemed determined to prove advanced stats were useless. Toronto's general manager, Dave Nonis, proclaimed, "People run with these stats like they're something we should pay attention to and make decisions on, and as of right now, very few of them are worth anything to us."

Nonis unloaded Toronto's speedy, skilled players, such as forward Mikhail Grabovski, in the offseason. Nonis decided to bring in a bunch of big, bruising players. The Maple Leafs' coach, Randy Carlyle, preferred a hard-hitting, defensive style of hockey. His players recorded lots of checks and pushed other teams around.

Toronto's tough guys stayed at the top of the standings for most of the season. But then they crashed—hard and fast. The Leafs lost 12 of their last 14 games, dropping from third place in the Eastern Conference to 12th. Predictions based on advanced stats came true.

Throughout the season, advanced stats analysts had been pointing to problems with the Maple Leafs possession and shot numbers. The Maple Leafs just didn't have the puck long enough or take enough shots to consistently win games. The team's hot start seemed to defy the odds, according to the statheads. Those experts predicted that the Leafs couldn't keep on winning without better numbers for puck possession and shots. Those experts were right.

It wasn't the first time advanced stats correctly predicted a late-season collapse. But forecasting the fall of the Maple Leafs kicked off the NHL's Summer of Analytics.

"I don't think there's any question about that," said Tyler Dellow. "The Leafs are a big deal, and Toronto is the center of the [hockey] universe. They raised the profile of the debate to a level that couldn't have happened anywhere else."

Perhaps the biggest surprise of the Summer of Analytics was that the Toronto Maple Leafs went all in on advanced stats. They hired multiple analysts and chose Kyle Dubas as assistant general manager. Dubas was just 28 years old at the time. He was, of course, a believer in hockey analytics.

▲ Kyle Dubas (right) and Leafs President Brendan Shanahan during the 2015 NHL Draft.

CHAPTER 3

INSIDE THE NUMBERS

▶ The Minnesota Wild tried to defy the odds in 2011–12, but the team became a prime example of how shot-based stats can predict success over a long season.

Numbers and statistics are the building blocks that advanced stats analysts use to build new ideas. The real challenge is stacking the building blocks into an accurate, useful concept.

Usually, it starts with the right question. How can we know if a team that starts off hot is the real deal? Who's the best goalie? What skills make a great penalty killer? Should the Edmonton Oilers have traded Wayne Gretzky to the L.A. Kings?

After asking the question, analysts take a deep dive into the statistics and try to forge a well-reasoned answer.

Shot-Based Statistics

What did the advanced stats analysts see in the numbers that told them the 2013–14 Maple Leafs weren't for real? Shots. It was all about shots.

The analytics community foretold the Maple Leafs collapse using shot-based statistics, like Corsi and Fenwick. Corsi and Fenwick are two similar modern stats. Both add up the shots a team takes and the shots their opponents take and compare them. (One difference: Fenwick doesn't count blocked shots.) If a team takes more shots than its opponents, advanced stats predict that the team should score more goals than opponents. This is because goals and shots have a clear statistical connection.

Why not just use goals? After all, hockey's plus-minus is a direct measurement of scoring. But it turns out plus-minus is a poor predictor—because goals don't occur very often. Goals don't have a large enough sample size to determine how well a team is playing.

The larger the sample size, the more accurate the result. If you took 10 slap shots from the blue line and put four of them in the net, your shooting percentage would be 40 percent. If you took 100 slap shots from the same spot and put 53 of them in the net, your shooting percentage would be 53 percent. The 53 percent would be a more accurate measurement of your true shooting percentage, because it is the result of a larger sample size.

In the middle of an NHL season, shots are typically a better measurement of a team than goals. The sample size of goals isn't large enough quite yet. Sometimes teams score more goals on fewer shots. Sometimes teams score fewer goals on more shots. But in-depth study shows that imbalances like those will last for only a short time. Eventually the number of shots a team takes and the number of goals it scores will return to the same statistical correlation.

That's why Corsi and Fenwick are a good way to predict how well a team is doing halfway through a season. A team might outscore their opponents at the beginning of a season and post a great record. But according to shot-based statistics, if that team is getting outshot regularly, its luck will run out sooner or later. The team will stop putting the puck in the net at a high rate, and its opponents will start scoring more goals.

Shot-based statistics proved especially insightful during the 2011–12 season. Although that may seem like ancient history now, it was a telling season in the world of hockey stats.

The Minnesota Wild raced out to a 20–8–5 record. The Kings started off so-so with a 14–14–4 record. Even though the Wild were atop the standings, the shot-based statistics predicted that the Wild were pretenders and the Kings were contenders.

At that point in the season, the Wild's Fenwick percentage was 0.426, and the Kings' was 0.513. That meant the Kings were getting 51.3 percent of the scoring chances (or all shots minus blocked shots) in their games. The Wild were getting just 42.6 percent of the scoring chances in their games.

A Corsi percentage or a Fenwick percentage over 50 is good. That shows the team is outshooting opponents. Because the Wild were being outshot by so much, advanced stats predicted that their winning ways were a mirage. The stats were right. The Wild ended that season with a 35–36–11 record and missed the playoffs. The Kings' high Fenwick numbers suggested that they were better than their early record. Right again. The Kings finished the regular season with a 40–27–15 record and went on to win the Stanley Cup.

The late collapses of the 2013–14 Maple Leafs and the 2011–12 Wild weren't the only ones predicted by shot-based statistics. The 2009–10 Colorado Avalanche had a 40–23–6 record and a terrible 45.5 percent Fenwick. They lost 10 of their last 13 games and squeaked into the playoffs. Then they were crushed by the San Jose Sharks. The 2010–11 Dallas Stars started off with a very impressive 29–13–5 record. However, their Fenwick was 46.5 percent. In their last 35 games, the Stars won just 13 and missed the playoffs

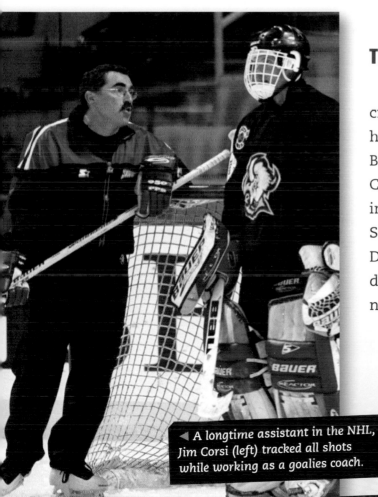

◀ A longtime assistant in the NHL, Jim Corsi (left) tracked all shots while working as a goalies coach.

The Story of Corsi

When Timothy Barnes created the Corsi statistic, he needed to name it. Barnes' inspiration for Corsi came from a radio interview with Buffalo Sabres General Manager, Darcy Regier. But "Regier" didn't seem right for the name of a stat.

Searching for a name, Barnes checked out the Sabres' website. While paging through photos of the Sabres' coaches, Barnes was taken by Jim Corsi and his memorable moustache.

Barnes named his new statistic Corsi. But the story doesn't end there. Amazingly, Jim Corsi, the Sabres' goalie coach, was already using a method very much like Barnes' stat.

Both men were adding up all shots, not just the official shots on goal. But Barnes and Corsi were using the statistic in a different way. Corsi was adding up only the shots against his team. He was using it as a way to measure the amount of pressure his goalies faced. Barnes counted both shots for and shots against. He compared the two statistics to figure out how well teams and players were playing.

The basic idea for the Corsi stat would never have reached Barnes without Jim Corsi, the man. "I always kidded Jim that he was the self-proclaimed protector of all goalies," Regier said. "He was always looking for a stat that would give his goalies their due. ... I can assure you, if I was on the radio talking about that sort of [statistical] stuff, it would have come from Jim."

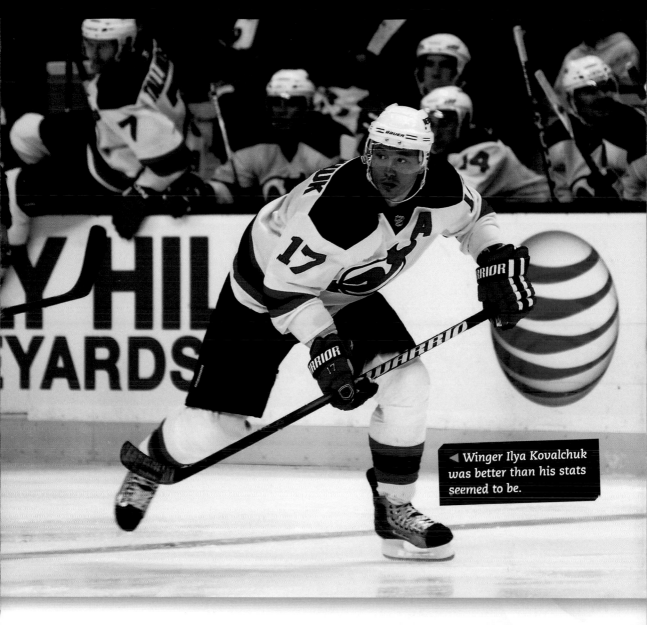

◀ Winger Ilya Kovalchuk was better than his stats seemed to be.

The Kovalchuk Mix-Up

Advanced stats analysts are usually the first to admit to their mistakes. Advanced stats were not kind to Ilya Kovalchuk, but they should have been. Kovalchuk was a rare NHL talent. However,

Kovalchuk's Corsi numbers were awful. The advanced stats crew branded Kovalchuk as an overpaid superstar. Today they admit they were wrong.

Analysts put too much value in Corsi numbers early on. Kovalchuk was one of the NHL's best shooters, a highly skilled sniper. His shooting percentage was 14.1 percent. That means in 100 shots, 14 of his found the back of the net. The league average is close to 9 percent.

Kovalchuk didn't have to take a bunch of shots to score. He was so good at putting the puck in the net that Corsi turned out to be a poor measurement for Kovalchuk. Analysts learned their lesson after they undervalued Kovalchuk. Now they don't rely only on Corsi (or Fenwick). They will take a good look at other statistics, like shooting percentage, before drawing their conclusions on a player.

Can We Just Have One Number, Please?

Hockey's advanced stats analysts have always looked to baseball's analytics movement for guidance. Baseball analytics are much further along than hockey analytics. The first *Bill James Baseball Abstract* was published in 1977, and it was groundbreaking. Hockey analytics didn't really start until the 21st century.

The baseball stat that advanced stats analysts crave is WAR, or Wins Above Replacement. WAR measures a baseball player's total value to the team. It calculates the number of wins a player adds to a team over a season compared to an average player in the league. In 2017 the Houston Astros' Jose Altuve had an 8.3 WAR. If the Astros had a league average second baseman, they would have lost about eight more games that season.

Hockey is a tricky game to wrap your analytical fingers around. The game hardly ever stops. Players come on and off the ice throughout a game. Goals don't happen very often. Add in power plays and penalty kills and you have a whole lot of factors to take in.

That doesn't mean the advanced stats crew hasn't tried. There are the Goals Versus Threshold (GVT), Total Hockey Rating (THoR), HERO Charts, and plenty more new stats. The formulas for these statistics can get very complex, like rocket-to-Mars complex. Despite the effort, hockey hasn't been able to come up with a widely accepted statistic like baseball's WAR.

CHAPTER 4

SHAPING THE GAME

▲ Wayne Gretzky (left) had a teammate whose job was to make sure no one took a cheap shot at the star.

The fourth line has been known by many names: the energy line, the grinding line, the enforcing line, or the checking line. Whatever the nickname, the fourth line's assignment is usually the same—body check the other team's offense into submission.

Traditionally, fourth-line players were large, physical players. They posed very little threat to score, but they did pose the threat of bodily harm to their opponents.

Advanced stats are changing the role of the fourth line and the type of players on NHL fourth lines. For years analysts asked why teams would use nothing but grinders and enforcers on the fourth line when more skilled players were available. Lately that message is getting through to some NHL teams. Fourth lines across the NHL have lost big, lumbering players in favor of faster, multi-skilled players.

Today the fourth line isn't the only part of the NHL changing because of advanced stats. In-depth study of stats is changing the shape of the game. Sometimes the changes aren't very welcome, but sometimes no one can argue with the numbers.

▲ Sidney Crosby's brilliant NHL career has been interrupted by concussions and other injuries.

Where Have All the Enforcers Gone?

There are some things you just don't do in a hockey game. These things include dirty hits, shooting the puck on a goalie after the whistle, and celebrating a goal when your team has a big lead. If you are guilty of one of these wrongdoings, a large man from the other team might pick a fight. If you don't fight him, you will become known as a "rat." Those are some old practices in pro hockey.

The unofficial rules about fighting in the NHL are known as "the code." This code is an unwritten but understood guide to how to play fairly and when to fight. The players that act as the police for the code are called enforcers. Fighting and some form of the code have always been a part of hockey and the NHL. However, fighting in the NHL is on the decline, and enforcers are disappearing from rosters. In the modern NHL, only a few teams carry old-fashioned enforcers.

Concerns about concussions have clearly helped reduce the number of enforcers. But advanced stats played a big role too. The advanced stats community never found any value in putting enforcers on the ice. The main concern of the stat crowd is figuring out how to win games.

And statistics show that enforcers don't help teams win games. Usually, the only stat an enforcer excels in is number of hits. The numbers show that enforcers don't even police the game as some people have claimed.

Analysts have compared the number of fights a team starts to the number of dirty hits and injuries a team suffers. There is no statistical evidence that supports the idea that enforcers protect their teammates from dirty hits and injuries.

The numbers paint a clear picture of the futility of fighting. Still, there is a lot of support for enforcers, especially among NHL players. Supporters insist that the value of enforcers can't be measured by any statistic. They claim that their sacrifice builds unity among their teammates, and their presence creates space and peace of mind for the goal scorers.

Some old-school types point to Sidney Crosby's career as proof of the necessity of enforcers. The Pittsburgh Penguins' superstar has missed more than 100 games due to concussions over the years. He has also played without an enforcer for most of his career.

Most of hockey's greatest goal scorers took the ice with an enforcer in their corner. Brett Hull had Kelly Chase with the St. Louis Blues. Steve Yzerman had Bob Probert and Joe Kocur with the Detroit Red Wings.

With the Oilers, Wayne Gretzky had Dave Semenko and Marty McSorle.

"You can tell guys 'til you're blue in the face that discipline and fining guys is going to work. Well, I already knew what the fine was for running Steve Yzerman in Detroit. If I did it, [the punishment] was Bob Probert and Joe Kocur. And I didn't do it," said former player Kelly Chase. "I didn't let guys on my team run at a great player because I was going to be the guy who inevitably paid the price."

The enforcer debate heated up again in the summer of 2017. The Penguins confounded the advanced stats community by acquiring tough-guy Ryan Reaves. The Penguins had won two straight Stanley Cups in 2016 and 2017. The analytics bunch didn't understand why they would need an enforcer. They had won two championships without one. Crosby welcomed his new, tough teammate. "When you get a player like that who is that tough it creates some room for guys," said Crosby.

It seems the debate over enforcers isn't over. It's easy to understand why superstars like Sidney Crosby like having a tough guy to watch over them. But it's hard to justify putting a big brawler on the ice if he doesn't bring any skills with him.

▲ Why drop the dump and chase? Because, many say, dumping the puck into an opponent's zone means losing possession. At best, dumping will lead to a scrap to regain puck control.

Get in the Zone

Sometimes advanced stats bring about a change that everyone can agree upon. This is the case with dump and chase. No one likes dump and chase hockey. Dump and chase usually ends up with a cluster of players jammed up against the boards, and that's no fun. It's boring to watch, and it doesn't look like the players enjoy it either.

Eric Tulsky, now an analyst for the Carolina Hurricanes, is responsible for a sharp decline of dump and chase. As a blogger for *Broad Street Hockey*, Tulsky focused attention on neutral-zone play. He wanted to find out the best way to move the puck from the neutral zone (between the blue lines) into the offensive zone.

In 2013, Tulsky submitted a paper titled "Using Zone Entry Data To Separate Offensive, Neutral, And Defensive Zone Performance" to the Massachusetts Institute of Technology Sloan Sports Analytics Conference. In the paper, Tulsky wrote, "It is found that talent for driving shot differential derives almost entirely from neutral zone play and that attack zone talent is largely confined to shot quality effects."

In other words, shot differential, which provides the basis of Corsi and Fenwick, depends on how teams play in the neutral zone. And for a team in possession of the puck in the neutral zone, its main goal is to take the puck across the blue line into the offensive zone. Tulsky stated that players who carry the puck into the offensive zone produce twice as much offense as players who dump and chase the puck.

The best teams in the NHL at the time, including the Blackhawks and the Kings, routinely carried the puck across the blue line. Because of Tulksy's paper, other teams took notice of their success and changed their tactics.

Mike Yeo, then the coach of the Minnesota Wild, decided to abandon the dump and chase before the 2013–14 season. Yeo's change in tactics was popular with his players. Wild winger and scoring leader Zach Parise said, "All you're doing is giving the puck away. I mean, it's so hard to get it, why would you give it away?"

Pretty soon, this idea was understood across the league. Today dump and chase is a last resort tactic, only used when nothing else is working.

The Shape of Hockey's Future

The move away from dump and chase happened before the Summer of Analytics. Back then, advances in the advanced stats community were public knowledge. Today talented advanced stats analysts, such as Eric Tulsky, work for NHL teams to create a competitive edge. Teams fiercely guard any breakthroughs their analysts come up with.

While a lot of analytics work is happening behind closed doors, there is a new crop of talented young analysts working as journalists. They try to keep the fans updated on the progress of advanced stats. And there are lots of analytic advances to come.

Compared to other sports, hockey statistics and analysis have a lot of catching up to do. But since the NHL opened its arms to advanced stats, hockey is changing and moving forward faster than ever. Advanced stats concepts are finally being put into play on the ice. If you don't mind a little change, it's going to be great fun to watch advanced stats shape hockey in the future.

STAT GLOSSARY

assist—a pass or touch of the puck that sets up a goal; up to two assists can be awarded on any goal

Corsi—also called shots attempted (SAT), this stat shows the difference between the number of attempted shots for and attempted shots against (including blocked shots) a team or a specific player when he's on the ice during even-strength situations

dump and chase—when teams send the puck into their offensive zone and attempt to regain possession through their forecheck

Fenwick—also called unblocked shots attempted (USAT), this is the difference between the number of attempted shots for and attempted shots against (excluding blocked shots) a team or a specific player when he's on the ice during even-strength situations

goals-against average (GAA)—the average number of goals allowed by a goaltender over a 60-minute time span

plus-minus (+/-)—the number of goals scored for a team minus the number scored against a team while a certain player is on the ice

point—any goal or assist

power-play percentage (PP%)—the success rate of a team's power play; found by dividing the number of times a team scores with the man advantage by the total number of power play opportunities

sample size—the number of pieces of data used in a statistical study; the larger the sample size, the more accurate the findings of the study

save percentage (SV%)—the percentage of pucks stopped by a goaltender; found by dividing a goalie's save total by the number of shots on goal he faced

shot differential—the difference between shots for and shots against

shot on goal—any shot at the goal that is either stopped by the goaltender or goes in for a goal; blocked shots and shots off the pipe that surrounds the net do not count

time on ice (TOI)—the total number of minutes a player plays in the game

READ MORE

Frederick, Shane. *Hockey's Record Breakers.* North Mankato, Minn.: Capstone Press, 2017.

McCollum, Sean. *Hockey's Best and Worst: A Guide to the Game's Good, Bad, and Ugly.* North Mankato, Minn.: Capstone Press, 2018.

Savage, Jeff. *Hockey Super Stats.* Minneapolis: Lerner Publications, 2017.

INTERNET SITES

Use FactHound to find internet sites related to this book.

Visit **www.facthound.com** Just type in 9781543514469 and go.

Check out projects, games and lots more at
www.capstonekids.com

INDEX